# Simple 1-2-3™

# EAGLE BRAND®

Publications International, Ltd.

Favorite Brand Name Recipes at www.fbnr.com

**Pictured on the front cover:** Banana Coconut Cream Pie *(page 46)*.

**Pictured on the back cover:** Choco-Peanut Butter-Brickle Cookies *(page 4)*.

ISBN-13: 978-1-4127-2655-9
ISBN-10: 1-4127-2655-7

Manufactured in China.

8 7 6 5 4 3 2 1

**Microwave Cooking:** Microwave ovens vary in wattage. Use the cooking
times as guidelines and check for doneness before adding more time.

**Preparation/Cooking Times:** Preparation times are based on the approximate
amount of time required to assemble the recipe before cooking, baking,
chilling or serving. These times include preparation steps such as measuring,
chopping and mixing. The fact that some preparations and cooking can be
done simultaneously is taken into account. Preparation of optional ingredients
and serving suggestions is not included.

# Contents

# Cookies

## Choco-Peanut Butter-Brickle Cookies

1 (14-ounce) can EAGLE BRAND® Sweetened Condensed Milk (NOT evaporated milk)
1 cup crunchy peanut butter
2 eggs
1 teaspoon vanilla extract
1½ cups all-purpose flour
1 teaspoon baking soda
½ teaspoon baking powder
½ teaspoon salt
1 cup (6 ounces) semisweet chocolate chips
1 cup chocolate-covered toffee bits or almond brickle chips

1. Preheat oven to 350°F. In large bowl, beat EAGLE BRAND®, peanut butter, eggs and vanilla until well blended.

2. In medium bowl, combine flour, baking soda, baking powder and salt. Add to peanut butter mixture; beat until blended. Stir in chocolate chips and toffee bits. Drop by heaping tablespoonfuls onto lightly greased baking sheets.

3. Bake 12 minutes or until lightly browned. Cool slightly on baking sheets; remove to wire racks to cool.

*Makes 3 dozen cookies*

**Prep Time:** *15 minutes*
**Bake Time:** *12 minutes*

# Cut-Out Cookies

**3½ cups all-purpose flour**
**2 teaspoons baking powder**
**¼ teaspoon salt**
**1 (14-ounce) can EAGLE BRAND® Sweetened Condensed Milk (NOT evaporated milk)**
**¾ cup (1½ sticks) butter or margarine, softened**
**2 eggs**
**1 tablespoon vanilla extract**
**Colored sugar sprinkles (optional)**
**Powdered Sugar Glaze (recipe follows, optional)**

1. In small bowl, combine flour, baking powder and salt. In large bowl with mixer on low speed, beat EAGLE BRAND®, butter, eggs and vanilla until just blended. Beat on medium speed 1 minute or until smooth. Add flour mixture; beat on low speed until blended. (If using hand-held mixer, use wooden spoon to add last portion of flour mixture.) Divide dough into thirds. Wrap and chill dough 2 hours or until easy to handle.

2. Preheat oven to 350°F. On lightly floured surface, roll out one portion of dough to ⅛-inch thickness. Cut out shapes. Gather dough and re-roll to use entire portion of dough. Repeat with remaining dough portions. Place cut-outs 1 inch apart on ungreased baking sheets. Sprinkle with colored sugar (optional). Bake 9 to 11 minutes, or until lightly browned around edges (do not overbake). Cool 5 minutes. Remove cookies to wire racks. When cool, glaze and decorate as desired. Store covered at room temperature. *Makes 5½ dozen cookies*

## Powdered Sugar Glaze

**2 cups sifted powdered sugar**
**½ teaspoon vanilla extract**
**2 tablespoons milk or whipping cream**
**Food coloring (optional)**

Whisk sugar and vanilla, adding just enough milk or cream to bind into a glaze consistency. Add food coloring (optional) to tint.

# Double Chocolate Cookies

1. Preheat oven to 350°F. In large bowl, combine all ingredients except white chocolate chips and nuts; beat until smooth. Stir in remaining ingredients.

2. Drop by rounded teaspoonfuls, 2 inches apart, onto ungreased baking sheets.

3. Bake 10 minutes or until tops are slightly crusted (do not overbake). Cool. Store tightly covered at room temperature.

*Makes about 3½ dozen cookies*

**Prep Time:** *15 minutes*
**Bake Time:** *10 minutes*

2 cups biscuit baking mix
1 (14-ounce) can EAGLE BRAND® Sweetened Condensed Milk (NOT evaporated milk)
8 (1-ounce) squares semisweet chocolate, melted *or* 1 (12-ounce) package semisweet chocolate chips, melted
3 tablespoons butter or margarine, melted
1 egg
1 teaspoon vanilla extract
1 cup (6 ounces) white chocolate chips
1 cup chopped nuts

# No-Bake Peanutty Chocolate Drops

½ cup (1 stick) butter or margarine
⅓ cup unsweetened cocoa
2½ cups quick-cooking oats
1 (14-ounce) can EAGLE BRAND® Sweetened Condensed Milk (NOT evaporated milk)
1 cup chopped peanuts
½ cup peanut butter

1. Line baking sheets with wax paper. In medium saucepan over medium heat, melt butter; stir in cocoa. Bring mixture to a boil.

2. Remove from heat; stir in remaining ingredients.

3. Drop by teaspoonfuls onto prepared baking sheets; chill 2 hours or until set. Store loosely covered in refrigerator.

*Makes about 5 dozen drops*

**Prep Time:** *10 minutes*
**Chill Time:** *2 hours*

# Chocolate Chip Treasure Cookies

1. Preheat oven to 375°F. In small bowl, combine graham cracker crumbs, flour and baking powder.

2. In large bowl, beat EAGLE BRAND® and butter until smooth. Add crumb mixture; mix well. Stir in chocolate chips, coconut and walnuts.

3. Drop by rounded tablespoonfuls onto ungreased baking sheets. Bake 9 to 10 minutes or until lightly browned. Cool. Store loosely covered at room temperature.

*Makes about 3 dozen cookies*

**Prep Time:** *15 minutes*
**Bake Time:** *9 to 10 minutes*

1½ cups graham cracker crumbs
½ cup all-purpose flour
2 teaspoons baking powder
1 (14-ounce) can EAGLE BRAND® Sweetened Condensed Milk (NOT evaporated milk)
½ cup (1 stick) butter or margarine, softened
2 cups (12 ounces) semisweet chocolate chips
1⅓ cups flaked coconut
1 cup chopped walnuts

# Coconut Macaroons

1. Preheat oven to 325°F. Line baking sheets with foil; grease and flour foil. Set aside.

2. In large bowl, combine EAGLE BRAND®, egg white, extracts and coconut; mix well. Drop by rounded teaspoonfuls onto prepared baking sheets; slightly flatten each mound with a spoon.

3. Bake 15 to 17 minutes or until lightly browned around edges. Immediately remove from baking sheets (macaroons will stick if allowed to cool on baking sheets); cool on wire racks. Store loosely covered at room temperature.

*Makes about 4 dozen cookies*

**Prep Time:** *10 minutes*
**Bake Time:** *15 to 17 minutes*

**1 (14-ounce) can EAGLE BRAND® Sweetened Condensed Milk (NOT evaporated milk)**
**1 egg white, whipped**
**2 teaspoons vanilla extract**
**1½ teaspoons almond extract**
**1 (14-ounce) package flaked coconut**

# Cinnamon Chip Gems

1. In large bowl, beat butter and cream cheese until well blended. Stir in flour, sugar and almonds. Cover; chill about 1 hour. Divide dough into 4 equal parts. Shape each part into 12 balls. Place each ball in small ungreased muffin cup (1¾ inches in diameter); press evenly on bottom and up side of each cup.

2. Preheat oven to 375°F. In small bowl, beat eggs. Add EAGLE BRAND® and vanilla; mix well. Place 7 cinnamon baking chips in bottom of each muffin cup; generously fill three-fourths full with EAGLE BRAND® mixture.

3. Bake 18 to 20 minutes or until tops are puffed and just beginning to turn golden brown. Cool 3 minutes. Sprinkle about 15 chips on top of filling. Cool completely in pan on wire rack. Remove from pan using small metal spatula or sharp knife. Cool completely. Store tightly covered at room temperature.

*Makes 4 dozen cookies*

Tip: For a pretty presentation, line the muffin pan with colorful paper baking cups before pressing the dough into the muffin cups.

1 cup (2 sticks) butter or margarine, softened
2 (3-ounce) packages cream cheese, softened
2 cups all-purpose flour
½ cup sugar
⅓ cup ground toasted almonds
2 eggs
1 (14-ounce) can EAGLE BRAND® Sweetened Condensed Milk (NOT evaporated milk)
1 teaspoon vanilla extract
1⅓ cups cinnamon baking chips, divided

# Easy Peanut Butter Cookies

1 (14-ounce) can EAGLE
   BRAND® Sweetened
   Condensed Milk
   (NOT evaporated milk)
1 to 1¼ cups peanut butter
1 egg
1 teaspoon vanilla extract
2 cups biscuit baking mix
   Granulated sugar

1. In large bowl, beat EAGLE BRAND®, peanut butter, egg and vanilla until smooth. Add biscuit mix; mix well. Chill at least 1 hour.

2. Preheat oven to 350°F. Shape dough into 1-inch balls. Roll in sugar. Place 2 inches apart on ungreased baking sheets. Flatten with fork in criss-cross pattern.

3. Bake 6 to 8 minutes or until lightly browned (do not overbake). Cool. Store tightly covered at room temperature.

*Makes about 5 dozen cookies*

Peanut Butter & Jelly Gems: Make dough as directed above. Shape into 1-inch balls and roll in sugar; do not flatten. Press thumb in center of each ball of dough; fill with jelly, jam or preserves. Proceed as directed above.

Any-Way-You-Like 'em Cookies: Stir 1 cup semisweet chocolate chips, chopped peanuts, raisins or flaked coconut into dough. Proceed as directed above.

# Macaroon Kisses

1. Preheat oven to 325°F. Line baking sheets with foil; grease and flour foil. Set aside.

2. In large bowl, combine EAGLE BRAND®, egg white, extracts and coconut; mix well. Drop by rounded teaspoonfuls onto prepared baking sheets; slightly flatten each mound with a spoon.

3. Bake 15 to 17 minutes or until lightly browned around edges. Remove from oven. Immediately press candy kiss, star or drop in center of each macaroon. Remove from baking sheets (macaroons will stick if allowed to cool on baking sheets); cool on wire racks. Store loosely covered at room temperature.

*Makes 4 dozen cookies*

1 (14-ounce) can EAGLE BRAND® Sweetened Condensed Milk (NOT evaporated milk)
1 egg white, whipped
2 teaspoons vanilla extract
1½ teaspoons almond extract
1 (14-ounce) package flaked coconut
48 solid milk chocolate candy kisses, stars or drops, unwrapped

# Chocolate Peanut Butter Chip Cookies

8 (1-ounce) squares semisweet chocolate
3 tablespoons butter or margarine
1 (14-ounce) can EAGLE BRAND® Sweetened Condensed Milk (NOT evaporated milk)
2 cups biscuit baking mix
1 egg
1 teaspoon vanilla extract
1 cup (6 ounces) peanut butter-flavored chips

1. Preheat oven to 350°F. In large saucepan over low heat, melt chocolate and butter with EAGLE BRAND®; remove from heat. Add biscuit mix, egg and vanilla; with mixer, beat until smooth and well blended.

2. Let mixture cool to room temperature. Stir in peanut butter chips. Shape into 1¼-inch balls. Place 2 inches apart on ungreased baking sheets. Bake 6 to 8 minutes or until tops are lightly crusty. Cool. Store tightly covered at room temperature.

*Makes about 4 dozen cookies*

**Prep Time:** *15 minutes*
**Bake Time:** *6 to 8 minutes*

# Peanut Butter Blossom Cookies

1. Preheat oven to 375°F. In large bowl, beat EAGLE BRAND® and peanut butter until smooth. Add biscuit mix and vanilla; mix well. Shape into 1-inch balls. Roll in sugar. Place 2 inches apart on ungreased baking sheets.

2. Bake 6 to 8 minutes or until lightly browned around edges (do not overbake). Remove from oven. Immediately press candy kiss in center of each cookie. Cool. Store tightly covered at room temperature.          *Makes about 5½ dozen cookies*

**Prep Time:** *15 minutes*
**Bake Time:** *6 to 8 minutes*

1 (14-ounce) can EAGLE BRAND® Sweetened Condensed Milk (NOT evaporated milk)
¾ cup peanut butter
2 cups biscuit baking mix
1 teaspoon vanilla extract
⅓ cup sugar
65 solid milk chocolate candy kisses, unwrapped

## Streusel Caramel Bars

2 cups all-purpose flour
¾ cup firmly packed light brown sugar
1 egg, beaten
¾ cup (1½ sticks) cold butter or margarine, divided
¾ cup chopped nuts
24 caramels, unwrapped
1 (14-ounce) can EAGLE BRAND® Sweetened Condensed Milk (NOT evaporated milk

1. Preheat oven to 350°F. In large bowl, combine flour, brown sugar and egg; cut in ½ cup butter until crumbly. Stir in nuts.

2. Reserve 2 cups crumb mixture. Press remaining crumb mixture firmly on bottom of greased 13×9-inch baking pan. Bake 15 minutes.

3. In heavy saucepan over low heat, melt caramels and remaining ¼ cup butter with EAGLE BRAND®. Pour over prepared crust. Top with reserved crumb mixture.

4. Bake 20 minutes or until bubbly. Cool. Cut into bars. Store loosely covered at room temperature.

*Makes 2 to 3 dozen bars*

**Prep Time:** *25 minutes*
**Bake Time:** *35 minutes*

# Pecan Pie Bars

2 cups all-purpose flour
¼ cup firmly packed brown sugar
½ cup (1 stick) cold butter
1½ cups chopped pecans
1 (14-ounce) can EAGLE BRAND® Sweetened Condensed Milk (NOT evaporated milk)
3 eggs, beaten
2 tablespoons lemon juice

1. Preheat oven to 350°F. In medium bowl, combine flour and brown sugar; cut in butter until crumbly.

2. Press mixture on bottom of 13×9-inch baking pan. Bake 10 to 15 minutes or until crust is light golden.

3. In large bowl, combine pecans, EAGLE BRAND®, eggs and lemon juice; pour over crust.

4. Bake 25 minutes or until filling is set. Cool. Cut into bars. Store covered at room temperature. *Makes about 3 dozen bars*

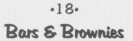

# S'More Bars

1. Preheat oven to 350°F (325°F for glass dish). In small bowl, combine graham cracker crumbs and butter; mix well. Press crumb mixture firmly on bottom of 13×9-inch baking pan.

2. Pour EAGLE BRAND® evenly over crumb mixture. Layer evenly with remaining ingredients; press down firmly with fork.

3. Bake 25 minutes or until lightly browned. Remove from oven; sprinkle with marshmallows. Return to oven. Bake 2 minutes more. Cool. Chill if desired. Cut into bars. Store covered at room temperature.

*Makes 2 to 3 dozen bars*

1½ cups graham cracker crumbs
½ cup (1 stick) butter or margarine
1 (14-ounce) can EAGLE BRAND® Sweetened Condensed Milk (NOT evaporated milk)
1 cup (6 ounces) milk chocolate or semisweet chocolate chips
1 cup chopped nuts (optional)
1 cup miniature marshmallows

# Lemon Crumb Bars

1 (18.25-ounce) package
   lemon or yellow cake
   mix
½ cup (1 stick) butter or
   margarine, softened
1 egg
2 cups finely crushed
   saltine crackers
1 (14-ounce) can EAGLE
   BRAND® Sweetened
   Condensed Milk
   (NOT evaporated milk)
½ cup lemon juice
3 egg yolks

1. Preheat oven to 350°F. In large bowl, combine cake mix, butter and 1 egg with mixer until crumbly. Stir in cracker crumbs. Reserve 2 cups crumb mixture. Press remaining crumb mixture firmly on bottom of greased 13×9-inch baking pan. Bake 15 to 20 minutes or until golden.

2. With mixer or wire whisk, beat EAGLE BRAND®, lemon juice and 3 egg yolks. Spread evenly over prepared crust. Top with reserved crumb mixture.

3. Bake 20 minutes longer or until set and top is golden. Cool. Cut into bars. Store covered in refrigerator.

*Makes 2 to 3 dozen bars*

**Prep Time:** *15 minutes*
**Bake Time:** *35 to 40 minutes*

# No-Bake Fudgy Brownies

1. Grease 8-inch square baking pan or line with foil; set aside.

2. In medium saucepan over low heat, combine EAGLE BRAND® and chocolate; cook and stir just until boiling. Reduce heat; cook and stir for 2 to 3 minutes more or until mixture thickens. Remove from heat; stir in vanilla.

3. Stir in 2 cups cookie crumbs. Spread evenly in prepared pan. Sprinkle with remaining cookie crumbs and chocolate pieces or nuts; press down gently with back of spoon.

4. Cover and chill 4 hours or until firm. Cut into squares. Store covered in refrigerator. *Makes 2 to 3 dozen bars*

***Prep Time:*** *10 minutes*
***Chill Time:*** *4 hours*

1 (14-ounce) can EAGLE BRAND® Sweetened Condensed Milk (NOT evaporated milk)
2 (1-ounce) squares unsweetened chocolate, chopped
1 teaspoon vanilla extract
2 cups plus 2 tablespoons packaged chocolate cookie crumbs, divided
¼ cup miniature candy-coated milk chocolate pieces or chopped nuts

# Golden Peanut Butter Bars

2 cups all-purpose flour
¾ cup firmly packed light
  brown sugar
1 egg, beaten
½ cup (1 stick) cold butter
  or margarine
1 cup finely chopped
  peanuts
1 (14-ounce) can EAGLE
  BRAND® Sweetened
  Condensed Milk
  (NOT evaporated milk)
½ cup peanut butter
1 teaspoon vanilla extract

1. Preheat oven to 350°F. In large bowl, combine flour, brown sugar and egg; cut in butter until crumbly. Stir in peanuts. Reserve 2 cups crumb mixture. Press remaining mixture on bottom of 13×9-inch baking pan. Bake 15 minutes or until lightly browned.

2. In large bowl, beat EAGLE BRAND®, peanut butter and vanilla. Spread over prepared crust; top with reserved crumb mixture.

3. Bake 25 minutes or until lightly browned. Cool. Cut into bars. Store covered at room temperature.      *Makes 2 to 3 dozen bars*

**Prep Time:** *20 minutes*
**Bake Time:** *40 minutes*

# Cheesecake-Topped Brownies

1. Preheat oven to 350°F. Prepare brownie mix as package directs. Spread in well-greased 13×9-inch baking pan.

2. In large bowl, beat cream cheese, butter and cornstarch until fluffy. Gradually beat in EAGLE BRAND®, egg and vanilla until smooth. Pour cheesecake mixture evenly over brownie batter.

3. Bake 45 minutes or until top is lightly browned. Cool. Spread with frosting (optional). Cut into bars. Store covered in refrigerator.                    *Makes 3 to 3½ dozen brownies*

**Prep Time:** *20 minutes*
**Bake Time:** *45 minutes*

1 (19.5- or 22-ounce, family size) package fudge brownie mix
1 (8-ounce) package cream cheese, softened
2 tablespoons butter or margarine, softened
1 tablespoon cornstarch
1 (14-ounce) can EAGLE BRAND® Sweetened Condensed Milk (NOT evaporated milk)
1 egg
2 teaspoons vanilla extract
Ready-to-spread chocolate frosting (optional)

# Candy Bar Bars

¾ cup (1½ sticks) butter or
    margarine, softened
¼ cup peanut butter
1 cup firmly packed light
    brown sugar
1 teaspoon baking soda
2 cups quick-cooking oats
1½ cups all-purpose flour
1 egg
1 (14-ounce) can EAGLE
    BRAND® Sweetened
    Condensed Milk
    (NOT evaporated milk)
4 cups chopped candy bars

1. Preheat oven to 350°F. In large bowl, combine butter and peanut butter. Add brown sugar and baking soda; beat well. Stir in oats and flour. Reserve 1¾ cups crumb mixture.

2. Stir egg into remaining crumb mixture; press firmly on bottom of ungreased 15×10-inch baking pan. Bake 15 minutes.

3. Pour EAGLE BRAND® evenly over baked crust. Stir together reserved crumb mixture and candy bar pieces; sprinkle evenly over top. Bake 25 minutes or until golden. Cool. Cut into bars. Store covered at room temperature. *Makes 4 dozen bars*

**Prep Time:** *15 minutes*
**Bake Time:** *40 minutes*

Tip: For this recipe, use your favorite candy bars, such as chocolate-covered caramel-topped nougat bars with peanuts, chocolate-covered crisp wafers, chocolate-covered caramel-topped cookie bars or chocolate-covered peanut butter cups.

# Magic Cookie Bars

1. Preheat oven to 350°F (325°F for glass baking dish). In small bowl, combine graham cracker crumbs and butter; mix well. Press crumb mixture firmly on bottom of 13×9-inch baking pan.

2. Pour EAGLE BRAND® evenly over crumb mixture. Layer evenly with remaining ingredients; press down firmly with fork.

3. Bake 25 minutes or until lightly browned. Cool. Chill if desired. Cut into bars or diamonds. Store covered at room temperature.  *Makes 2 to 3 dozen bars*

**Prep Time:** *10 minutes*
**Bake Time:** *25 minutes*

7-Layer Magic Cookie Bars: Substitute 1 cup (6 ounces) butterscotch-flavored chips for 1 cup semisweet chocolate chips. (Peanut butter-flavored chips or white chocolate chips can be substituted for butterscotch-flavored chips.)

Magic Peanut Cookie Bars: Substitute 2 cups (about ¾ pound) chocolate-covered peanuts for semisweet chocolate chips and chopped nuts.

Magic Rainbow Cookie Bars: Substitute 2 cups plain candy-coated chocolate pieces for semisweet chocolate chips.

**1½ cups graham cracker crumbs**
**½ cup (1 stick) butter or margarine, melted**
**1 (14-ounce) can EAGLE BRAND® Sweetened Condensed Milk (NOT evaporated milk)**
**2 cups (12 ounces) semisweet chocolate chips**
**1⅓ cups flaked coconut**
**1 cup chopped nuts**

# Toffee-Top Cheesecake Bars

1¼ cups all-purpose flour
1 cup powdered sugar
½ cup unsweetened cocoa
¼ teaspoon baking soda
¾ cup (1½ sticks) butter or
    margarine
1 (8-ounce) package cream
    cheese, softened
1 (14-ounce) can EAGLE
    BRAND® Sweetened
    Condensed Milk
    (NOT evaporated milk)
2 eggs
1 teaspoon vanilla extract
1½ cups (8-ounce package)
    English toffee bits,
    divided

1. Preheat oven to 350°F. In medium bowl, combine flour, powdered sugar, cocoa and baking soda; cut in butter until mixture is crumbly. Press firmly on bottom of ungreased 13×9-inch baking pan. Bake 15 minutes.

2. In large bowl, beat cream cheese until fluffy. Add EAGLE BRAND®, eggs and vanilla; beat until smooth. Stir in 1 cup English toffee bits. Pour mixture over hot crust. Bake 25 minutes or until set and edges just begin to brown.

3. Cool 15 minutes. Sprinkle remaining ½ cup English toffee bits evenly over top. Cool completely. Refrigerate several hours or until cold. Store covered in refrigerator.

*Makes about 3 dozen bars*

**Prep Time:** *20 minutes*
**Bake Time:** *40 minutes*

# Brownie Raspberry Bars

1. Preheat oven to 350°F. In heavy saucepan, over low heat, melt chocolate chips with butter.

2. In large bowl, combine melted chocolate chips, biscuit mix, EAGLE BRAND®, egg and vanilla; mix well. Stir in nuts. Spread in well-greased 15×10-inch baking pan. Bake 20 minutes or until center is set. Cool completely.

3. In small bowl, beat cream cheese, sugar, jam and food coloring (optional) until smooth; spread over brownies. Garnish with Chocolate Drizzle. Chill. Cut into bars. Store covered in refrigerator.

*Makes 3 to 4 dozen bars*

Chocolate Drizzle: In heavy saucepan over low heat, melt ½ cup semisweet chocolate chips with 1 tablespoon shortening. Immediately drizzle over bars.

1 cup (6 ounces) semisweet chocolate chips
¼ cup (½ stick) butter or margarine
2 cups biscuit baking mix
1 (14-ounce) can EAGLE BRAND® Sweetened Condensed Milk (NOT evaporated milk)
1 egg
1 teaspoon vanilla extract
1 cup chopped nuts
1 (8-ounce) package cream cheese, softened
½ cup powdered sugar
½ cup red raspberry jam
Red food coloring (optional)
Chocolate Drizzle (recipe follows)

# White Chocolate Squares

2 cups (12 ounces) white chocolate chips, divided
¼ cup (½ stick) butter or margarine
2 cups all-purpose flour
½ teaspoon baking powder
1 (14-ounce) can EAGLE BRAND® Sweetened Condensed Milk (NOT evaporated milk)
1 egg
1 teaspoon vanilla extract
1 cup chopped pecans, toasted
Powdered sugar

1. Preheat oven to 350°F. In large saucepan over low heat, melt 1 cup white chocolate chips and butter. Stir in flour and baking powder until blended. Stir in EAGLE BRAND®, egg and vanilla. Stir in pecans and remaining white chocolate chips. Spoon mixture into greased 13×9-inch baking pan.

2. Bake 20 to 25 minutes. Cool. Sprinkle with powdered sugar; cut into squares. Store covered at room temperature.

*Makes 2 dozen squares*

*Prep Time: 15 minutes*
*Bake Time: 20 to 25 minutes*

# Chocolate Almond Bars

1. Preheat oven to 350°F. In large bowl, combine flour and sugar; cut in butter until crumbly. Press firmly on bottom of ungreased 13×9-inch baking pan. Bake 20 minutes or until lightly browned.

2. In medium saucepan over low heat, melt 1 cup chocolate chips with EAGLE BRAND®. Remove from heat; cool slightly. Beat in egg. Stir in almonds and extract. Spread over baked crust. Bake 25 minutes or until set. Cool.

3. Melt remaining ½ cup chocolate chips with shortening; drizzle over bars. Chill 10 minutes or until set. Cut into bars. Store covered at room temperature.          *Makes 2 to 3 dozen bars*

1½ cups all-purpose flour
⅔ cup sugar
¾ cup (1½ sticks) cold
   butter or margarine
1½ cups semisweet chocolate
   chips, divided
1 (14-ounce) can EAGLE
   BRAND® Sweetened
   Condensed Milk
   (NOT evaporated milk)
1 egg
2 cups almonds, toasted
   and chopped
½ teaspoon almond extract
1 teaspoon solid shortening

# Cookie Pizza

1 (18-ounce) package refrigerated sugar cookie dough

2 cups (12 ounces) semisweet chocolate chips

1 (14-ounce) can EAGLE BRAND® Sweetened Condensed Milk (NOT evaporated milk)

2 cups candy-coated milk chocolate pieces

2 cups miniature marshmallows

½ cup peanuts

1. Preheat oven to 375°F. Divide cookie dough in half; press each half onto ungreased 12-inch pizza pan. Bake 10 minutes or until golden. Remove from oven.

2. In heavy saucepan over low heat, melt chocolate chips with EAGLE BRAND®. Spread over crusts. Sprinkle with chocolate pieces, marshmallows and peanuts.

3. Bake 4 minutes or until marshmallows are lightly toasted. Cool. Cut into wedges.              *Makes 2 pizzas (24 servings)*

**Prep Time:** *15 minutes*
**Bake Time:** *14 minutes*

*Bars & Brownies*

# Fudge Topped Brownies

1. Preheat oven to 350°F. In large bowl, combine sugar, butter, flour, cocoa, baking powder, eggs, milk and 1½ teaspoons vanilla; mix well. Stir in nuts (optional). Spread in greased 13×9-inch baking pan. Bake 40 minutes or until brownies begin to pull away from sides of pan.

2. In heavy saucepan over low heat, melt chocolate chips with EAGLE BRAND®, remaining 1½ teaspoons vanilla and salt. Remove from heat. Immediately spread over hot brownies. Cool. Chill. Cut into bars. Store covered at room temperature.

*Makes 3 to 3½ dozen brownies*

2 cups sugar
1 cup (2 sticks) butter or margarine, melted
1 cup all-purpose flour
⅔ cup unsweetened cocoa
½ teaspoon baking powder
2 eggs
½ cup milk
3 teaspoons vanilla extract, divided
1 cup chopped nuts (optional)
2 cups (12 ounces) semisweet chocolate chips
1 (14-ounce) can EAGLE BRAND® Sweetened Condensed Milk (NOT evaporated milk)
Dash salt

# Cheesecakes

## Chocolate Raspberry Cheesecake

2 (3-ounce) packages cream cheese, softened
1 (14-ounce) can EAGLE BRAND® Sweetened Condensed Milk (NOT evaporated milk)
1 egg
3 tablespoons lemon juice
1 teaspoon vanilla extract
1 cup fresh or frozen raspberries
1 (6-ounce) prepared chocolate crumb pie crust
Chocolate Glaze (recipe follows)

1. Preheat oven to 350°F. In medium bowl, beat cream cheese until fluffy. Gradually beat in EAGLE BRAND® until smooth. Add egg, lemon juice and vanilla; mix well.

2. Arrange raspberries on bottom of crust. Slowly pour cheese mixture over fruit.

3. Bake 30 to 35 minutes or until center is almost set. Cool.

4. Prepare Chocolate Glaze and spread over cheesecake; chill. Garnish as desired. Store covered in refrigerator.

*Makes one cheesecake*

Chocolate Glaze: In small saucepan, over low heat, melt 2 (1-ounce) squares semisweet chocolate with ¼ cup whipping cream. Cook and stir until thickened and smooth. Remove from heat; cool slightly.

**Prep Time:** *20 minutes*
**Bake Time:** *30 to 35 minutes*

# Chocolate Chip Cheesecake

1½ cups finely crushed
    creme-filled chocolate
    sandwich cookie
    crumbs (18 cookies)
2 to 3 tablespoons butter
    or margarine, melted
3 (8-ounce) packages
    cream cheese, softened
1 (14-ounce) can EAGLE
    BRAND® Sweetened
    Condensed Milk
    (NOT evaporated milk)
3 eggs
2 teaspoons vanilla extract
1 cup (6 ounces) miniature
    semisweet chocolate
    chips, divided
1 teaspoon all-purpose
    flour

1. Preheat oven to 300°F. In small bowl, mix cookie crumbs and butter; press firmly on bottom of ungreased 9-inch springform pan.

2. In large bowl, beat cream cheese until fluffy. Gradually beat in EAGLE BRAND® until smooth. Add eggs and vanilla; mix well.

3. In small bowl, toss ½ cup chocolate chips with flour to coat; stir into cheese mixture. Pour into prepared pan. Sprinkle remaining ½ cup chocolate chips evenly over top.

4. Bake 55 to 60 minutes or until set. Cool. Chill. Garnish as desired. Store covered in refrigerator.

*Makes one (9-inch) cheesecake*

Tip: For the best distribution of the chocolate chips throughout this cheesecake, do not oversoften or overbeat the cream cheese.

# Chocolate Mint Cheesecake Bars

1. Preheat oven to 325°F. In medium bowl, combine cookie crumbs and butter; blend well. Press crumb mixture firmly on bottom of ungreased 9-inch baking pan. Bake 6 minutes. Cool.

2. In medium bowl, beat cream cheese until fluffy. Gradually beat in EAGLE BRAND®, eggs and peppermint extract until smooth. Pour over cooled cookie base. Bake 25 to 30 minutes. Cool 20 minutes; chill.

3. Just before serving, in heavy saucepan over low heat, melt chocolate chips and shortening. Drizzle over chilled cheesecake bars. Sprinkle with chopped chocolate mint candies. Cut into bars. Store covered in refrigerator.     *Makes 1½ to 2 dozen bars*

2 cups finely crushed creme-filled chocolate sandwich cookie crumbs (24 cookies)
½ cup (1 stick) butter or margarine, melted
1 (8-ounce) package cream cheese, softened
1 (14-ounce) can EAGLE BRAND® Sweetened Condensed Milk (NOT evaporated milk)
2 eggs
1 tablespoon peppermint extract
½ cup semisweet chocolate chips
2 teaspoons shortening
14 crème de menthe thin candies, chopped

# Maple Pumpkin Cheesecake

1¼ cups graham cracker crumbs
¼ cup sugar
¼ cup (½ stick) butter or margarine, melted
3 (8-ounce) packages cream cheese, softened
1 (14-ounce) can EAGLE BRAND® Sweetened Condensed Milk (NOT evaporated milk)
1 (15-ounce) can pumpkin (2 cups)
3 eggs
¼ cup pure maple syrup
1½ teaspoons ground cinnamon
1 teaspoon ground nutmeg
½ teaspoon salt
Maple Pecan Glaze (recipe follows)

1. Preheat oven to 325°F. In small bowl, combine graham cracker crumbs, sugar and butter; press firmly on bottom of ungreased 9-inch springform pan.

2. In large bowl, beat cream cheese until fluffy. Gradually beat in EAGLE BRAND® until smooth. Add pumpkin, eggs, maple syrup, cinnamon, nutmeg and salt; mix well. Pour into prepared crust.

3. Bake 1 hour 15 minutes or until center appears nearly set when shaken. Cool 1 hour. Cover and chill at least 4 hours. Top with Maple Pecan Glaze. Store covered in refrigerator.

*Makes one (9-inch) cheesecake*

Maple Pecan Glaze: In medium saucepan over medium-high heat, combine 1 cup (½ pint) whipping cream and ¾ cup pure maple syrup; bring to a boil. Boil rapidly 15 to 20 minutes or until thickened, stirring occasionally. Add ½ cup chopped pecans. Cover and chill until served. Stir before serving.

**Prep Time:** *25 minutes*
**Bake Time:** *1 hour and 15 minutes*
**Cool Time:** *1 hour*
**Chill Time:** *4 hours*

Cheesecakes

# Creamy Baked Cheesecake

1. Preheat oven to 300°F. In small bowl, combine graham cracker crumbs, sugar and butter; press firmly on bottom of ungreased 9-inch springform pan.

2. In large bowl, beat cream cheese until fluffy. Gradually beat in EAGLE BRAND® until smooth. Add eggs and lemon juice; mix well. Pour into prepared crust.

3. Bake 50 to 55 minutes or until set. Remove from oven; top with sour cream. Bake 5 minutes longer. Cool. Chill. Prepare Raspberry Topping (optional) and serve with cheesecake. Store covered in refrigerator.           *Makes one (9-inch) cheesecake*

## Raspberry Topping

    2 cups water
    ½ cup powdered sugar
    ¼ cup red raspberry jam
    1 tablespoon cornstarch
    1 cup frozen red raspberries

In small saucepan over medium heat, combine water, powdered sugar, jam and cornstarch. Cook and stir until thickened and clear. Cool. Stir in raspberries.

1¼ cups graham cracker crumbs
¼ cup sugar
⅓ cup (⅔ stick) butter or margarine, melted
2 (8-ounce) packages cream cheese, softened
1 (14-ounce) can EAGLE BRAND® Sweetened Condensed Milk (NOT evaporated milk)
3 eggs
¼ cup lemon juice
1 (8-ounce) container sour cream, at room temperature
Raspberry Topping (recipe follows, optional)

# Black & White Cheesecake

2 (3-ounce) packages
    cream cheese, softened
1 (14-ounce) can EAGLE
    BRAND® Sweetened
    Condensed Milk
    (NOT evaporated milk)
1 egg
1 teaspoon vanilla extract
½ cup miniature semisweet
    chocolate chips
1 teaspoon all-purpose
    flour
1 (6-ounce) prepared
    chocolate crumb pie
    crust
  Chocolate Glaze (recipe
    follows)

1. Preheat oven to 350°F. In medium bowl, beat cream cheese until fluffy. Gradually beat in EAGLE BRAND® until smooth. Add egg and vanilla; mix well.

2. In small bowl, toss chocolate chips with flour to coat; stir into cream cheese mixture. Pour into crust.

3. Bake 35 minutes or until center springs back when lightly touched. Cool. Prepare Chocolate Glaze and spread over cheesecake. Chill. Store covered in refrigerator.

*Makes one cheesecake*

Chocolate Glaze: In small saucepan over low heat, melt ½ cup miniature semisweet chocolate chips with ¼ cup whipping cream. Cook and stir until thickened and smooth. Use immediately.

**Prep Time:** *15 minutes*
**Bake Time:** *35 minutes*

*Cheesecakes*

# Mini Cheesecakes

1. Preheat oven to 300°F. In small bowl, combine graham cracker crumbs, sugar and butter; press equal portions firmly on bottoms of 24 lightly greased or foil-lined muffin cups.

2. In large bowl, beat cream cheese until fluffy. Gradually beat in EAGLE BRAND® until smooth. Add eggs and vanilla; mix well. Spoon equal amounts of mixture (about 3 tablespoons) into prepared cups. Bake 20 minutes or until cheesecakes spring back when lightly touched. Cool.* Chill. Garnish as desired. Store covered in refrigerator.      *Makes 2 dozen mini cheesecakes*

*If greased muffin cups are used, cool baked cheesecakes. Freeze 15 minutes; remove with narrow spatula. Proceed as directed above.*

**Prep Time:** *20 minutes*
**Bake Time:** *20 minutes*

Chocolate Mini Cheesecakes: Melt 1 cup (6 ounces) semisweet chocolate chips; mix into batter. Proceed as directed above, baking 20 to 25 minutes.

1½ **cups graham cracker or chocolate wafer cookie crumbs**
¼ **cup sugar**
¼ **cup (½ stick) butter or margarine, melted**
3 **(8-ounce) packages cream cheese, softened**
1 **(14-ounce) can EAGLE BRAND® Sweetened Condensed Milk (NOT evaporated milk)**
3 **eggs**
2 **teaspoons vanilla extract**

# Almond Praline Cheesecake

¾ cup graham cracker
    crumbs
½ cup slivered almonds,
    toasted and finely
    chopped
¼ cup firmly packed brown
    sugar
¼ cup (½ stick) butter or
    margarine, melted
3 (8-ounce) packages
    cream cheese, softened
1 (14-ounce) can EAGLE
    BRAND® Sweetened
    Condensed Milk
    (NOT evaporated milk)
3 eggs
1 teaspoon almond extract
    Almond Praline Topping
    (recipe follows)

1. Preheat oven to 300°F. In medium bowl, mix graham cracker crumbs, almonds, brown sugar and butter; press on bottom of ungreased 9-inch springform pan or 13×9-inch baking pan.

2. In large bowl, beat cream cheese until fluffy. Gradually beat in EAGLE BRAND® until smooth. Add eggs and almond extract; mix well. Pour into prepared crust.

3. Bake 55 to 60 minutes or until center is set. Cool. Top with Almond Praline Topping. Chill. Store covered in refrigerator.

*Makes one (9-inch) cheesecake*

## Almond Praline Topping

⅓ cup firmly packed dark brown sugar
⅓ cup whipping cream
½ cup chopped toasted slivered almonds

In small saucepan over medium heat, combine brown sugar and cream. Cook and stir until sugar dissolves. Simmer 5 minutes or until thickened. Remove from heat; add almonds. Spoon evenly over cheesecake. (To make topping for 13×9-inch pan, double all topping ingredients; simmer 10 to 12 minutes or until thickened.)

# Frozen Mocha Cheesecake Loaf

1. Line 9×5-inch loaf pan with foil, extending foil over sides of pan. In small bowl, combine cookie crumbs and butter; press firmly on bottom and halfway up sides of prepared pan.

2. In large bowl, beat cream cheese until fluffy. Gradually beat in EAGLE BRAND® until smooth; add vanilla. Fold in whipped cream.

3. Remove half the mixture and place in medium bowl; fold in coffee mixture and chocolate syrup. Spoon half the chocolate mixture into prepared crust, then half the vanilla mixture. Repeat. With table knife, cut through cream mixture to marble.

4. Cover; freeze 6 hours or until firm. To serve, remove from pan; peel off foil. Cut into slices and garnish as desired. Store covered in freezer. *Makes 8 to 10 servings*

**Prep Time:** *20 minutes*
**Freeze Time:** *6 hours*

**2 cups finely crushed creme-filled chocolate sandwich cookies (24 cookies)**
**3 tablespoons butter or margarine, melted**
**1 (8-ounce) package cream cheese, softened**
**1 (14-ounce) can EAGLE BRAND® Sweetened Condensed Milk (NOT evaporated milk)**
**1 tablespoon vanilla extract**
**2 cups (1 pint) whipping cream, whipped**
**2 tablespoons instant coffee dissolved in 1 tablespoon hot water**
**½ cup chocolate-flavored syrup**

# Black Forest Chocolate Cheesecake

1½ cups chocolate wafer cookie crumbs

3 tablespoons butter or margarine, melted

2 (1-ounce) squares unsweetened chocolate

1 (14-ounce) can EAGLE BRAND® Sweetened Condensed Milk (NOT evaporated milk)

2 (8-ounce) packages cream cheese, softened

3 eggs

3 tablespoons cornstarch

1 teaspoon almond extract

1 (21-ounce) can cherry pie filling, chilled

1. Preheat oven to 300°F. In small bowl, combine cookie crumbs and butter; press firmly on bottom of 9-inch springform pan.

2. In small saucepan over low heat, melt chocolate with EAGLE BRAND®, stirring constantly. Remove from heat.

3. In large bowl, beat cream cheese until fluffy. Gradually beat in EAGLE BRAND® mixture until smooth. Add eggs, cornstarch and almond extract; mix well. Pour into prepared pan.

4. Bake 50 to 55 minutes or until center is set. Cool and chill overnight. Top with cherry pie filling before serving. Store covered in refrigerator. *Makes one (9-inch) cheesecake*

# Frozen Peppermint Cheesecake

1. In medium bowl, combine cookie crumbs and sugar. Add butter; mix well. Line 9-inch round cake or springform pan with foil. Press 2 cups crumb mixture firmly on bottom and halfway up side of prepared pan. Chill.

2. In large bowl, beat cream cheese until fluffy. Gradually beat in EAGLE BRAND® until smooth. Stir in peppermint extract and food coloring (optional); mix well. Fold in whipped cream. Pour filling into prepared pan. Cover; freeze 6 hours or until firm. Garnish with topping (optional). Store covered in freezer.

*Makes one (9-inch) cheesecake*

2 cups chocolate wafer cookie or sandwich cookie crumbs
¼ cup sugar
¼ cup (½ stick) butter or margarine, melted
1 (8-ounce) package cream cheese, softened
1 (14-ounce) can EAGLE BRAND® Sweetened Condensed Milk (NOT evaporated milk)
2 teaspoons peppermint extract
Red food coloring (optional)
2 cups whipping cream, whipped
Hot fudge ice cream topping (optional)

## Two-Tone Cheesecake Bars

2 cups finely crushed creme-filled chocolate sandwich cookie crumbs (24 cookies)
3 tablespoons butter or margarine, melted
3 (8-ounce) packages cream cheese, softened
1 (14-ounce) can EAGLE BRAND® Sweetened Condensed Milk (NOT evaporated milk)
3 eggs
2 teaspoons vanilla extract
2 (1-ounce) squares unsweetened chocolate, melted
Chocolate Glaze (recipe follows)

1. Preheat oven to 300°F. In medium bowl, mix cookie crumbs and butter; press firmly on bottom of ungreased 13×9-inch baking pan.

2. In large bowl, beat cream cheese until fluffy. Gradually beat in EAGLE BRAND® until smooth. Add eggs and vanilla; mix well. Pour half the batter evenly over prepared crust. Stir melted chocolate into remaining batter; pour evenly over plain batter.

3. Bake 55 to 60 minutes or until set. Cool. Top with Chocolate Glaze. Chill. Cut into bars. Store covered in refrigerator.

*Makes 2 to 3 dozen bars*

### Chocolate Glaze

2 (1-ounce) squares unsweetened chocolate
2 tablespoons butter or margarine
Pinch salt
1¾ cups powdered sugar
3 tablespoons hot water or cream

In heavy saucepan over low heat, melt chocolate and butter with salt. Remove from heat. Add powdered sugar and hot water or cream; mix well. Immediately spread over cheesecake.

# Raspberry Swirl Cheesecakes

1. Preheat oven to 350°F. In blender container, blend 1½ cups raspberries until smooth; press through sieve to remove seeds. Stir ⅓ cup EAGLE BRAND® into raspberry purée; set aside.

2. In large bowl, beat cream cheese, eggs and remaining EAGLE BRAND® until smooth. Spoon into crusts. Drizzle with raspberry mixture. With table knife, gently swirl raspberry mixture through cream cheese mixture.

3. Bake 25 minutes or until centers are nearly set when shaken. Cool. Cover and chill at least 4 hours. Garnish with chocolate leaves and fresh raspberries (optional). Store covered in refrigerator.

*Makes two cheesecakes*

Chocolate Leaves: Place 1 (1-ounce) square semisweet or white chocolate in microwave-safe bowl. Microwave at HIGH (100% power) 1 to 2 minutes, stirring every minute until smooth. With small, clean paintbrush, paint several coats of melted chocolate on undersides of nontoxic leaves, such as mint, lemon or strawberry. Wipe off any chocolate from top sides of leaves. Place leaves, chocolate sides up, on wax-paper-lined baking sheet or on curved surface, such as rolling pin. Refrigerate leaves until chocolate is firm. To use, carefully peel leaves away from chocolate.

1½ cups fresh or frozen red raspberries, thawed
1 (14-ounce) can EAGLE BRAND® Sweetened Condensed Milk (NOT evaporated milk), divided
2 (8-ounce) packages cream cheese, softened
3 eggs
2 (6-ounce) prepared chocolate crumb pie crusts
Chocolate and white chocolate leaves (optional)
Fresh raspberries for garnish (optional)

## Banana Coconut Cream Pie

3 tablespoons cornstarch
1⅓ cups water
1 (14-ounce) can EAGLE
    BRAND® Sweetened
    Condensed Milk
    (NOT evaporated milk)
3 egg yolks, beaten
2 tablespoons butter or
    margarine
1 teaspoon vanilla extract
½ cup flaked coconut,
    toasted
2 medium bananas
2 tablespoons lemon juice
1 (9-inch) prepared graham
    cracker or baked pie
    crust
    Whipped cream and
    additional toasted
    coconut (optional)

1. In heavy saucepan over medium heat, dissolve cornstarch in water; stir in EAGLE BRAND® and egg yolks. Cook and stir until thickened and bubbly. Remove from heat; add butter and vanilla. Cool slightly. Fold in coconut; set aside.

2. Peel and slice bananas into ¼-inch-thick rounds. Toss banana slices gently with lemon juice; drain. Arrange bananas on bottom of crust. Pour filling over bananas.

3. Cover; refrigerate 4 hours or until set. Top with whipped cream and toasted coconut (optional). Store covered in refrigerator.

*Makes one (9-inch) pie*

# Double Chocolate Ice Cream Squares

1½ cups finely crushed
    creme-filled chocolate
    sandwich cookie
    crumbs (18 cookies)
2 to 3 tablespoons butter
    or margarine, melted
1 (14-ounce) can EAGLE
    BRAND® Sweetened
    Condensed Milk
    (NOT evaporated milk)
3 (1-ounce) squares
    unsweetened
    chocolate, melted
2 teaspoons vanilla extract
1 cup chopped nuts
    (optional)
2 cups (1 pint) whipping
    cream, whipped
Whipped topping

1. In medium bowl, combine cookie crumbs and butter; press firmly on bottom of ungreased 13×9-inch baking pan.

2. In large bowl, beat EAGLE BRAND®, melted chocolate and vanilla until well blended. Stir in nuts (optional). Fold in whipped cream. Pour into prepared crust. Spread with whipped topping. Cover; freeze 6 hours or until firm. Garnish with additional finely chopped nuts or as desired. Store covered in freezer.

*Makes about 1 dozen squares*

Rocky Road Ice Cream Squares: Substitute chopped peanuts for nuts; add 1 cup miniature marshmallows to EAGLE BRAND® mixture. Proceed as directed above.

# Fudgy Pecan Pie

1. Preheat oven to 350°F. In medium saucepan over low heat, melt butter and chocolate. Stir in EAGLE BRAND®, hot water and eggs; mix well. Remove from heat; stir in pecans, vanilla and salt. Pour into crust.

2. Bake 40 to 45 minutes or until center is set. Cool slightly. Serve warm or chilled. Garnish as desired. Store covered in refrigerator.

*Makes one (9-inch) pie*

**Prep Time:** *15 minutes*
**Bake Time:** *40 to 45 minutes*

¼ cup (½ stick) butter or margarine
2 (1-ounce) squares unsweetened chocolate
1 (14-ounce) can EAGLE BRAND® Sweetened Condensed Milk (NOT evaporated milk)
½ cup hot water
2 eggs, well beaten
1¼ cups pecan halves or pieces
1 teaspoon vanilla extract
⅛ teaspoon salt
1 (9-inch) unbaked pie crust

# Blueberry Streusel Cobbler

1 pint fresh or frozen
   blueberries
1 (14-ounce) can EAGLE
   BRAND® Sweetened
   Condensed Milk
   (NOT evaporated milk)
2 teaspoons grated lemon
   zest
¾ cup plus 2 tablespoons
   cold butter or
   margarine, divided
2 cups biscuit baking mix,
   divided
½ cup firmly packed light
   brown sugar
½ cup chopped nuts
   Vanilla ice cream
   Blueberry Sauce (recipe
   follows)

1. Preheat oven to 325°F. In medium bowl, combine blueberries, EAGLE BRAND® and lemon zest.

2. In large bowl, cut ¾ cup butter into 1½ cups biscuit mix until crumbly; stir in blueberry mixture. Spread in greased 9-inch square baking pan.

3. In small bowl, combine remaining ½ cup biscuit mix and brown sugar; cut in remaining 2 tablespoons butter until crumbly. Add nuts. Sprinkle over batter.

4. Bake 65 to 70 minutes. Serve warm with vanilla ice cream and Blueberry Sauce. Store covered in refrigerator.

*Makes 8 to 12 servings*

Blueberry Sauce: **In saucepan over medium heat, combine ½ cup granulated sugar, 1 tablespoon cornstarch, ½ teaspoon ground cinnamon and ¼ teaspoon ground nutmeg. Gradually add ½ cup water. Cook and stir until thickened. Stir in 1 pint blueberries; cook and stir until hot.**

***Prep Time:*** *15 minutes*
***Bake Time:*** *1 hour and 10 minutes*

# Creamy Caramel Flan

1. Preheat oven to 350°F. In heavy skillet over medium heat, cook and stir sugar until melted and caramel-colored. Carefully pour into 8 ungreased 6-ounce custard cups, tilting to coat bottoms.

2. In large bowl, beat eggs; stir in water, EAGLE BRAND®, vanilla and salt. Pour into prepared custard cups. Set cups in large shallow pan. Fill pan with 1 inch hot water.

3. Bake 25 minutes or until knife inserted near centers comes out clean. Move cups from larger pan to wire rack. Cool 1 hour. Chill several hours or overnight. To serve, loosen sides of flans with knife; invert flans onto individual serving plates. Top with Sugar Garnish (optional), or garnish as desired. Store covered in refrigerator.

*Makes 8 servings*

Sugar Garnish: Fill medium metal bowl half-full of ice. In medium saucepan over medium-high heat, combine 1 cup sugar with ¼ cup water. Stir; cover and bring to a boil. Cook over high heat 5 to 6 minutes or until light brown in color. Immediately place pan in ice for 1 minute. Using spoon, carefully drizzle sugar decoratively over foil. Cool. To serve, peel sugar garnish from foil.

**Prep Time:** *15 minutes*
**Bake Time:** *25 minutes*

¾ cup sugar
4 eggs
1¾ cups water
1 (14-ounce) can EAGLE BRAND® Sweetened Condensed Milk (NOT evaporated milk)
1 teaspoon vanilla extract
⅛ teaspoon salt
Sugar Garnish (recipe follows, optional)

# Cranberry Crumb Pie

1 (9-inch) unbaked pie
  crust
1 (8-ounce) package cream
  cheese, softened
1 (14-ounce) can EAGLE
  BRAND® Sweetened
  Condensed Milk
  (NOT evaporated milk)
¼ cup lemon juice
3 tablespoons light brown
  sugar, divided
2 tablespoons cornstarch
1 (16-ounce) can whole
  berry cranberry sauce
⅓ cup all-purpose flour
¼ cup (½ stick) cold butter
  or margarine
¾ cup chopped walnuts

1. Preheat oven to 425°F. Bake pie crust 6 minutes; remove from oven. Reduce oven temperature to 375°F.

2. In large bowl, beat cream cheese until fluffy. Gradually beat in EAGLE BRAND® until smooth. Stir in lemon juice. Pour into baked crust.

3. In small bowl, combine 1 tablespoon brown sugar and cornstarch; mix well. Stir in cranberry sauce. Spoon evenly over cheese mixture.

4. In medium bowl, cut butter into flour and remaining 2 tablespoons brown sugar until crumbly. Stir in walnuts. Sprinkle evenly over cranberry mixture. Bake 45 to 50 minutes or until bubbly and golden. Cool. Serve at room temperature or chill thoroughly. Store covered in refrigerator.

*Makes one (9-inch) pie*

Desserts

# Cool and Minty Party Cake

1. Line 9-inch round cake pan with foil. In large bowl, combine EAGLE BRAND®, peppermint extract and food coloring (optional). Fold in whipped cream. Pour into prepared pan; cover. Freeze at least 6 hours or until firm.

2. Prepare and bake cake mix as package directs for two 9-inch round layers. Remove from pans; cool completely.

3. With fork, poke holes in cake layers, 1 inch apart, halfway through each layer. Spoon small amounts of liqueur into holes. Place one cake layer on serving plate; top with frozen EAGLE BRAND® mixture, then second cake layer. Trim frozen layer to edge of cake layers.

4. Frost quickly with whipped topping. Return to freezer for at least 6 hours before serving. Garnish as desired. Store covered in freezer.

*Makes one (9-inch) cake*

1 (14-ounce) can EAGLE BRAND® Sweetened Condensed Milk (NOT evaporated milk)

2 teaspoons peppermint extract

8 drops green food coloring (optional)

2 cups (1 pint) whipping cream, whipped (do not use non-dairy whipped topping)

1 (18.25- or 18.5-ounce) package white cake mix, plus ingredients to prepare mix

Green crème de menthe liqueur

1 (8-ounce) container frozen non-dairy whipped topping, thawed

# Chocolate Cream Crêpes

1 (14-ounce) can EAGLE BRAND® Sweetened Condensed Milk (NOT evaporated milk)
¼ cup cold water
1 (4-serving-size) package instant chocolate pudding and pie filling mix
¼ cup unsweetened cocoa
1 cup (½ pint) whipping cream, whipped
1 (4½-ounce) package ready-to-use crêpes (10 crêpes)
1½ cups sliced fresh fruit such as peaches, berries or kiwifruit
Powdered sugar
White chocolate curls (optional)

1. In large bowl, with mixer, beat EAGLE BRAND® and water. Beat in pudding mix and cocoa. Fold in whipped cream. Cover and chill 15 minutes.

2. Pipe or spoon generous ⅓ cup filling down center of each crêpe. Roll up each crêpe. Place on serving plate. Spoon fruit over crêpes. Sprinkle with powdered sugar. Garnish with white chocolate curls (optional). Store covered in refrigerator.

*Makes 5 servings*

**Prep Time:** *10 minutes plus assembling*
**Chill Time:** *15 minutes*

# Peach Cream Cake

1. Cut cake into ¼-inch slices; arrange half the slices on bottom of ungreased 13×9-inch baking dish.

2. In large bowl, combine EAGLE BRAND®, water and almond extract. Add pudding mix; beat well. Chill 5 minutes.

3. Fold in whipped cream. Spread half the cream mixture over cake slices; arrange half the peach slices on top. Top with remaining cake slices, cream filling and peach slices.

4. Chill 4 hours or until set. Cut into squares to serve. Store covered in refrigerator.    *Makes one (13×9-inch) cake*

1 (10¾-ounce) loaf angel food cake, frozen
1 (14-ounce) can EAGLE BRAND® Sweetened Condensed Milk (NOT evaporated milk)
1 cup cold water
1 teaspoon almond extract
1 (4-serving-size) package instant vanilla pudding mix
2 cups (1 pint) whipping cream, whipped
4 cups sliced peeled fresh peaches (about 2 pounds)

# Chocolate Truffle Pie

1 envelope unflavored
    gelatin
½ cup water
3 (1-ounce) squares
    unsweetened or
    semisweet chocolate,
    melted and cooled
1 (14-ounce) can EAGLE
    BRAND® Sweetened
    Condensed Milk
    (NOT evaporated milk)
1 teaspoon vanilla extract
2 cups (1 pint) whipping
    cream, whipped
1 (6-ounce) prepared
    chocolate crumb pie
    crust

1. In small saucepan, sprinkle gelatin over water; let stand 1 minute. Over low heat, stir until gelatin dissolves. Cool.

2. In large bowl, beat chocolate and EAGLE BRAND® until smooth. Stir in gelatin mixture and vanilla. Fold in whipped cream. Pour into prepared crust.

3. Chill 3 hours or until set. Garnish as desired. Store covered in refrigerator.                    *Makes one pie*

# Ambrosia Freeze

1. In large bowl with electric mixer on low speed, beat cream cheese and bananas until nearly smooth. Beat in EAGLE BRAND®, yogurt and lemon juice. Stir in orange sections, pineapple and coconut. Stir in food coloring (optional). Spoon into ungreased 11×7-inch baking dish. Cover and freeze 6 hours or until firm.

2. Remove from freezer 15 minutes before serving. Cut into 1×1-inch cubes; serve in stemmed glasses or dessert dishes.

*Makes 8 to 10 servings*

1 (8-ounce) container strawberry cream cheese
2 medium bananas, mashed
1 (14-ounce) can EAGLE BRAND® Sweetened Condensed Milk (NOT evaporated milk)
1 (8-ounce) container low-fat strawberry yogurt
2 tablespoons lemon juice
1 (11-ounce) can mandarin orange sections, drained
1 (8-ounce) can crushed pineapple, well drained
½ cup toasted flaked coconut
Red food coloring (optional)

Desserts

# Rich Caramel Cake

1 (14-ounce) package
  caramels, unwrapped
½ cup (1 stick) butter or
  margarine
1 (14-ounce) can EAGLE
  BRAND® Sweetened
  Condensed Milk
  (NOT evaporated milk)
1 (18.25- or 18.5-ounce)
  package chocolate
  cake mix, plus
  ingredients to prepare
  mix
1 cup coarsely chopped
  pecans

1. Preheat oven to 350°F. In heavy saucepan over low heat, melt caramels and butter. Remove from heat; add EAGLE BRAND®. Mix well; set aside. Prepare cake mix as package directs.

2. Spread 2 cups cake batter into greased 13×9-inch baking pan; bake 15 minutes. Spread caramel mixture evenly over cake; spread remaining cake batter over caramel mixture. Top with pecans. Bake 30 to 35 minutes or until cake springs back when lightly touched. Cool.                    *Makes 10 to 12 servings*

Desserts

# Lemon Icebox Pie

1. In medium bowl, combine EAGLE BRAND®, lemon juice and food coloring (optional). Fold in whipped cream.

2. Pour into prepared crust. Chill 3 hours or until set. Garnish as desired. Store covered in refrigerator.     *Makes one (9-inch) pie*

1 (14-ounce) can EAGLE BRAND® Sweetened Condensed Milk (NOT evaporated milk)
½ cup lemon juice
   Yellow food coloring (optional)
1 cup (½ pint) whipping cream, whipped
1 (6-ounce) prepared graham cracker or baked pie crust

# Strawberries & Cream Dessert

1 (14-ounce) can EAGLE BRAND® Sweetened Condensed Milk (NOT evaporated milk)

1½ cups cold water

1 (4-serving-size) package instant vanilla pudding and pie filling mix

2 cups (1 pint) whipping cream, whipped

1 (12-ounce) prepared loaf pound cake, cut into cubes (about 6 cups)

4 cups sliced fresh strawberries

½ cup strawberry preserves

Additional sliced fresh strawberries

Toasted slivered almonds

1. In large bowl, combine EAGLE BRAND® and water; mix well. Add pudding mix; beat until well blended. Chill 5 minutes. Fold in whipped cream.

2. Spoon 2 cups pudding mixture into 4-quart round glass serving bowl; top with half the cake cubes, half the strawberries, half the preserves and half the remaining pudding mixture. Repeat layers of cake cubes, strawberries and preserves; top with remaining pudding mixture. Garnish with additional strawberries and almonds. Chill 4 hours or until set. Store covered in refrigerator.

*Makes 10 to 12 servings*

Variation: Here is another way to layer this spectacular dessert: Spoon 2 cups pudding mixture into 4-quart round glass serving bowl; top with cake cubes, all of the strawberries, all of the preserves and the remaining pudding mixture. Garnish and chill as directed above.

# German Chocolate Cake

1. Preheat oven to 350°F. In large bowl, combine cake mix, water, 3 eggs, oil and ⅓ cup EAGLE BRAND®. Beat on low speed until moistened; then beat on high speed 2 minutes.

2. Pour into well-greased and floured 13×9-inch baking pan. Bake 40 to 45 minutes or until toothpick inserted near center comes out clean.

3. In small saucepan over low heat, combine remaining EAGLE BRAND®, butter and egg yolk. Cook and stir until thickened, about 6 minutes. Add pecans, coconut and vanilla; spread over warm cake. Store covered in refrigerator.

*Makes 10 to 12 servings*

**Prep Time:** *15 minutes*
**Bake Time:** *40 to 45 minutes*

1 (18.25- or 18.5-ounce) package German chocolate cake mix
1 cup water
3 eggs, plus 1 egg yolk
½ cup vegetable oil
1 (14-ounce) can EAGLE BRAND® Sweetened Condensed Milk (NOT evaporated milk), divided
3 tablespoons butter or margarine
1 egg yolk
⅓ cup chopped pecans
⅓ cup flaked coconut
1 teaspoon vanilla extract

# Perfect Pumpkin Pie

1 (15-ounce) can pumpkin
(about 2 cups)
1 (14-ounce) can EAGLE
BRAND® Sweetened
Condensed Milk
(NOT evaporated milk)
2 eggs
1 teaspoon ground
cinnamon
½ teaspoon ground ginger
½ teaspoon ground nutmeg
½ teaspoon salt
1 (9-inch) unbaked pie
crust

1. Preheat oven to 425°F. In medium bowl, beat pumpkin, EAGLE BRAND®, eggs, spices and salt until smooth. Pour into crust. Bake 15 minutes.

2. Reduce oven temperature to 350°F and continue baking 35 to 40 minutes longer or until knife inserted 1 inch from crust comes out clean. Cool. Garnish as desired. Store covered in refrigerator.

*Makes one (9-inch) pie*

Sour Cream Topping: In medium bowl, combine 1½ cups sour cream, 2 tablespoons sugar and 1 teaspoon vanilla extract. After pie has baked 30 minutes at 350°F, spread mixture evenly over top; bake 10 minutes.

Streusel Topping: In medium bowl, combine ½ cup packed brown sugar and ½ cup all-purpose flour; cut in ¼ cup (½ stick) cold butter or margarine until crumbly. Stir in ¼ cup chopped nuts. After pie has baked 30 minutes at 350°F, sprinkle streusel evenly over top; bake 10 minutes.

Chocolate Glaze: In small saucepan over low heat, melt ½ cup semisweet chocolate chips and 1 teaspoon solid shortening. Drizzle or spread over top of baked pie.

# Tiramisu

1. In small bowl, dissolve coffee crystals in water; reserve 1 tablespoon coffee mixture. Brush remaining coffee mixture on cut sides of ladyfingers; set aside.

2. In large bowl, beat ¾ cup EAGLE BRAND® and mascarpone. Add 1¼ cups whipping cream, vanilla and reserved 1 tablespoon coffee mixture; beat until soft peaks form. Fold in ½ cup chocolate chips.

3. In heavy saucepan over low heat, melt remaining ½ cup chocolate chips with remaining EAGLE BRAND®.

4. In 8 tall dessert glasses or parfait glasses, layer mascarpone mixture, chocolate mixture and ladyfinger pieces, beginning and ending with mascarpone mixture. Cover and chill at least 4 hours.

5. In medium bowl, beat remaining ¾ cup cream until soft peaks form. To serve, spoon whipped cream over dessert. Garnish as desired. Store covered in refrigerator.          *Makes 8 servings*

2 tablespoons instant coffee crystals
½ cup hot water
2 (3-ounce) packages ladyfingers (24), cut crosswise into quarters
1 (14-ounce) can EAGLE BRAND® Sweetened Condensed Milk (NOT evaporated milk), divided
8 ounces mascarpone or cream cheese, softened
2 cups (1 pint) whipping cream, divided
1 teaspoon vanilla extract
1 cup (6 ounces) miniature semisweet chocolate chips, divided
Grated semisweet chocolate and/or strawberries (optional)

## Rocky Road Candy

**2 cups (12 ounces) semisweet chocolate chips**
**2 tablespoons butter or margarine**
**1 (14-ounce) can EAGLE BRAND® Sweetened Condensed Milk (NOT evaporated milk)**
**2 cups dry-roasted peanuts**
**1 (10½-ounce) package miniature marshmallows**

1. Line 13×9-inch baking pan with wax paper. In heavy saucepan over low heat, melt chocolate chips and butter with EAGLE BRAND®; remove from heat.

2. In large bowl, combine peanuts and marshmallows; stir in chocolate mixture. Spread in prepared pan. Chill 2 hours or until firm.

3. Remove candy from pan; peel off paper and cut into squares. Store loosely covered at room temperature.

*Makes about 3½ dozen candies*

**Prep Time:** *10 minutes*
**Chill Time:** *2 hours*

Microwave Method: In 1-quart glass measure, combine chocolate chips, butter and EAGLE BRAND®. Cook at HIGH (100% power) 3 minutes, stirring after 1½ minutes. Stir to melt chips. Let stand 5 minutes. Proceed as directed above.

# White Christmas Jewel Fudge

3 cups premium white chocolate chips
1 (14-ounce) can EAGLE BRAND® Sweetened Condensed Milk (NOT evaporated milk)
1½ teaspoons vanilla extract
⅛ teaspoon salt
½ cup chopped green candied cherries
½ cup chopped red candied cherries

1. In heavy saucepan over low heat, melt white chocolate chips with EAGLE BRAND®, vanilla and salt. Remove from heat; stir in cherries. Spread evenly in wax-paper-lined 8- or 9-inch square pan. Chill 2 hours or until firm.

2. Turn fudge onto cutting board; peel off paper and cut into squares. Store covered in refrigerator.

*Makes 2¼ pounds fudge*

Tip: Fudge makes a great homemade holiday gift!

# Chocolate Raspberry Truffles

1. In large microwave-safe bowl, combine EAGLE BRAND®, liqueur, butter and jam. Microwave at HIGH (100% power) 3 minutes.

2. Stir in chocolate chips until smooth. Cover and chill 1 hour.

3. Shape mixture into 1-inch balls; roll in powdered sugar or almonds. Store covered at room temperature.

*Makes 4 dozen truffles*

**Prep Time:** *10 minutes*
**Cook Time:** *3 minutes*
**Chill Time:** *1 hour*

1 (14-ounce) can EAGLE BRAND® Sweetened Condensed Milk (NOT evaporated milk)
¼ cup raspberry liqueur
2 tablespoons butter or margarine
2 tablespoons seedless raspberry jam
2 cups (12 ounces) semisweet chocolate chips
½ cup powdered sugar or finely chopped toasted almonds

Treats

# Creamy Hot Chocolate

**1 (14-ounce) can EAGLE BRAND® Sweetened Condensed Milk (NOT evaporated milk)**
**½ cup unsweetened cocoa**
**1½ teaspoons vanilla extract**
**⅛ teaspoon salt**
**6½ cups hot water**
**Mini marshmallows (optional)**

1. In large saucepan over medium heat, combine EAGLE BRAND®, cocoa, vanilla and salt; mix well.

2. Slowly stir in water. Heat through, stirring occasionally. Do not boil. Top with marshmallows (optional). Store covered in refrigerator.          *Makes about 2 quarts hot chocolate*

**Prep Time:** *8 to 10 minutes*

Microwave Method: In 2-quart glass measure, combine all ingredients except marshmallows. Microwave at HIGH (100% power) 8 to 10 minutes, stirring every 3 minutes. Top with marshmallows (optional). Store covered in refrigerator.

Tip: Hot chocolate can be stored in the refrigerator for up to 5 days. Mix well and reheat before serving.

# Layered Mint Chocolate Fudge

1. In heavy saucepan over low heat, melt semisweet chocolate chips with 1 cup EAGLE BRAND®. Stir in vanilla. Spread half the mixture into wax-paper-lined 8- or 9-inch square pan; chill 10 minutes or until firm. Keep remaining chocolate mixture at room temperature.

2. In heavy saucepan over low heat, melt white chocolate chips with remaining EAGLE BRAND®. (Mixture will be thick.) Add peppermint extract and food coloring (optional). Spread over chilled chocolate layer; chill 10 minutes longer or until firm.

3. Spread reserved chocolate mixture over mint layer. Chill 2 hours or until firm. Turn fudge onto cutting board; peel off paper and cut into squares. Store covered in refrigerator.

*Makes about 1¾ pounds fudge*

**Prep Time:** *20 minutes*
**Chill Time:** *2 hours 20 minutes*

**2 cups (12 ounces) semisweet chocolate chips**
**1 (14-ounce) can EAGLE BRAND® Sweetened Condensed Milk (NOT evaporated milk), divided**
**2 teaspoons vanilla extract**
**1 cup (6 ounces) premium white chocolate chips *or* 6 ounces vanilla-flavored candy coating***
**1 tablespoon peppermint extract**
**Green or red food coloring (optional)**

*\*Also called confectionery coating or almond bark. If it is not available in your local supermarket, it can be purchased in candy specialty stores.*

# Strawberry Splash Punch

1½ cups fresh whole
    strawberries
½ cup lemon juice, chilled
1 (14-ounce) can EAGLE
    BRAND® Sweetened
    Condensed Milk
    (NOT evaporated
    milk), chilled
1 (1-liter) bottle
    strawberry-flavored
    carbonated beverage,
    chilled
  Ice cubes (optional)
  Fresh whole strawberries
    (optional)

1. In blender container, combine 1½ cups strawberries and lemon juice; cover and blend until smooth.

2. Add EAGLE BRAND®; cover and blend. Pour into large pitcher. Gradually stir in carbonated beverage. Add ice (optional). Garnish each serving with whole strawberry (optional).

*Makes 10 servings*

**Prep Time:** *10 minutes*

Treats

# Candy Crunch

1. Line 15×10-inch baking pan with foil. Place pretzels in large bowl.

2. In large saucepan over low heat, melt chips with EAGLE BRAND®. Cook, stirring constantly, until smooth. Pour over pretzels, stirring to coat.

3. Immediately spread mixture in prepared pan. Sprinkle with dried fruit; press down lightly with back of spoon. Chill 1 to 2 hours or until set. Break into chunks. Store loosely covered at room temperature. *Makes about 1¾ pounds candy*

**Prep Time:** *10 minutes*
**Chill Time:** *1 to 2 hours*

4 cups (half of 15-ounce bag) pretzel sticks or pretzel twists
4 cups (24 ounces) white chocolate chips
1 (14-ounce) can EAGLE BRAND® Sweetened Condensed Milk (NOT evaporated milk)
1 cup dried fruit, such as dried cranberries, raisins or mixed dried fruit bits

# Peanut Butter Blocks

1 (14-ounce) can EAGLE
BRAND® Sweetened
Condensed Milk
(NOT evaporated milk)
1¼ cups creamy peanut
butter
⅓ cup water
1 tablespoon vanilla extract
½ teaspoon salt
1 cup cornstarch, sifted
1 pound vanilla-flavored
candy coating*
2 cups peanuts, finely
chopped

*Also called confectionery coating or
almond bark. If it is not available in
your local supermarket, it can be
purchased in candy specialty stores.

1. In heavy saucepan, combine EAGLE BRAND®, peanut butter, water, vanilla and salt; stir in cornstarch. Over medium heat, cook and stir until thickened and smooth.

2. Add candy coating; cook and stir until melted and smooth. Spread evenly in wax-paper-lined 9-inch square baking pan. Chill 2 hours or until firm. Cut into squares; roll firmly in peanuts to coat. Store covered at room temperature or in refrigerator.

*Makes about 3 pounds candy*

**Prep Time:** *15 minutes*
**Chill Time:** *2 hours*

Microwave Method: In 1-quart glass measure, combine EAGLE BRAND®, peanut butter, water, vanilla and salt; stir in cornstarch. Microwave at HIGH (100% power) 2 minutes; mix well. In 2-quart glass measure, melt candy coating at MEDIUM (50% power) 3 to 5 minutes, stirring after each minute. Add peanut butter mixture; mix well. Proceed as directed above.

# Fruit Smoothies

1. In blender container, combine chilled EAGLE BRAND®, yogurt, banana, whole strawberries, pineapple with its juice and lemon juice; cover and blend until smooth.

2. With blender running, gradually add ice cubes, blending until smooth. Garnish with strawberries (optional). Serve immediately.

*Makes 5 servings*

**Prep Time:** *5 minutes*

Peach Smoothies: Omit strawberries and pineapple. Add 2 cups frozen or fresh sliced peaches. Proceed as directed above.

Key Lime Smoothies: Omit strawberries, pineapple and lemon juice. Add ⅓ cup key lime juice from concentrate. Proceed as directed above. Tint with green food coloring, if desired. Garnish with lime slices, if desired.

1 (14-ounce) can EAGLE BRAND® Sweetened Condensed Milk (NOT evaporated milk), chilled
1 (8-ounce) carton plain yogurt
1 small banana, cut up
1 cup frozen or fresh whole strawberries
1 (8-ounce) can crushed pineapple packed in juice, chilled
2 tablespoons lemon juice
1 cup ice cubes
  Additional fresh strawberries (optional)

# White Truffles

**2 pounds vanilla-flavored candy coating\***

**1 (14-ounce) can EAGLE BRAND® Sweetened Condensed Milk (NOT evaporated milk)**

**1 tablespoon vanilla extract**

**1 pound chocolate-flavored candy coating,\* melted, or unsweetened cocoa**

*\*Also called confectionery coating or almond bark. If it is not available in your local supermarket, it can be purchased in candy specialty stores.*

1. In heavy saucepan over low heat, melt vanilla candy coating with EAGLE BRAND®. Remove from heat; stir in vanilla. Cool.

2. Shape into 1-inch balls. With toothpick, partially dip each ball into melted chocolate candy coating or roll in cocoa. Place on wax-paper-lined baking sheets until firm. Store covered in refrigerator.                              *Makes about 8 dozen truffles*

Flavoring Options: **Amaretto:** Omit vanilla. Add 3 tablespoons amaretto or other almond-flavored liqueur and ½ teaspoon almond extract. Roll in finely chopped toasted almonds. **Orange:** Omit vanilla. Add 3 tablespoons orange-flavored liqueur. Roll in finely chopped toasted almonds mixed with finely grated orange peel. **Rum:** Omit vanilla. Add ¼ cup dark rum. Roll in flaked coconut. **Bourbon:** Omit vanilla. Add 3 tablespoons bourbon. Roll in finely chopped toasted nuts.

# Festive Fudge

1. In heavy saucepan over low heat, melt chocolate chips with EAGLE BRAND® and salt. Remove from heat; stir in nuts (optional) and vanilla. Spread evenly into wax-paper-lined 8- or 9-inch square pan. Chill 2 hours or until firm.

2. Turn fudge onto cutting board; peel off paper and cut into squares. Store covered in refrigerator.

*Makes about 2 pounds fudge*

Chocolate Peanut Butter Chip Glazed Fudge: Substitute ¾ cup peanut butter chips for nuts. For glaze, melt additional ½ cup peanut butter chips with ½ cup whipping cream; stir until thick and smooth. Spread over fudge.

Marshmallow Fudge: Add 2 tablespoons butter to chocolate mixture. Substitute 2 cups miniature marshmallows for nuts.

**3 cups (18 ounces) semisweet or milk chocolate chips**
**1 (14-ounce) can EAGLE BRAND® Sweetened Condensed Milk (NOT evaporated milk)**
**Dash salt**
**½ to 1 cup chopped nuts (optional)**
**1½ teaspoons vanilla extract**

# Chilled Café Latte

**2 tablespoons instant coffee**
**¾ cup warm water**
**1 (14-ounce) can EAGLE BRAND® Fat Free or Original Sweetened Condensed Milk (NOT evaporated milk)**
**1 teaspoon vanilla extract**
**4 cups ice cubes**

1. In blender container, dissolve coffee in water. Add EAGLE BRAND® and vanilla; blend on high speed until well blended.

2. Gradually add ice to blender, blending until smooth. Serve immediately. Store covered in refrigerator.

*Makes 4 servings or about 5 cups latte*

# Strawberry Bon Bons

1. In large bowl, combine EAGLE BRAND®, coconut, almonds, ⅓ cup gelatin, almond extract and enough red food coloring to tint mixture to desired strawberry red shade. Transfer mixture to food processor and pulse several times to form paste. Chill until firm enough to handle. Shape spoonfuls of coconut mixture (about ¾ tablespoon) into strawberry shapes.

2. Sprinkle remaining gelatin on flat dish; roll each strawberry in gelatin to coat. Place on wax-paper-lined baking sheet; chill.

3. To make frosting "hulls," combine powdered sugar, whipping cream and green food coloring until well blended. Fill pastry bag fitted with open star tip with frosting; pipe small amount on top of each strawberry to form hull. Store tightly covered in refrigerator.

*Makes about 2½ pounds or about 4 dozen candies*

1 (14-ounce) can EAGLE BRAND® Sweetened Condensed Milk (NOT evaporated milk)
1 (14-ounce) package flaked coconut
1 cup ground blanched almonds
1 (6-ounce) package strawberry-flavored gelatin
1 teaspoon almond extract
Red food coloring
2 cups powdered sugar
½ cup whipping cream
Green food coloring

# Festive Cranberry Cream Punch

Cranberry Ice Ring
(recipe follows) or ice
1 (14-ounce) can EAGLE
BRAND® Sweetened
Condensed Milk
(NOT evaporated milk)
1 (12-ounce) can frozen
cranberry juice
cocktail concentrate,
thawed
1 cup cranberry-flavored
liqueur (optional)
Red food coloring
(optional)
2 (1-liter) bottles club soda
or ginger ale, chilled

1. Prepare Cranberry Ice Ring one day in advance.

2. In punch bowl, combine EAGLE BRAND®, cranberry concentrate, liqueur (optional) and food coloring (optional).

3. Just before serving, add club soda and Cranberry Ice Ring or ice. Store tightly covered in refrigerator.

*Makes about 3 quarts punch*

## Cranberry Ice Ring

2 cups cranberry juice cocktail
1½ cups water
¾ to 1 cup cranberries and lime slices or mint leaves

Combine cranberry juice cocktail and water. In 1½-quart ring mold, pour ½ cup cranberry liquid. Arrange cranberries and lime slices or mint leaves in mold; freeze. Add remaining 3 cups cranberry liquid to mold; freeze overnight.

# Index

# Metric Conversion Chart

## VOLUME MEASUREMENTS (dry)

1/8 teaspoon = 0.5 mL
1/4 teaspoon = 1 mL
1/2 teaspoon = 2 mL
3/4 teaspoon = 4 mL
1 teaspoon = 5 mL
1 tablespoon = 15 mL
2 tablespoons = 30 mL
1/4 cup = 60 mL
1/3 cup = 75 mL
1/2 cup = 125 mL
2/3 cup = 150 mL
3/4 cup = 175 mL
1 cup = 250 mL
2 cups = 1 pint = 500 mL
3 cups = 750 mL
4 cups = 1 quart = 1 L

## VOLUME MEASUREMENTS (fluid)

1 fluid ounce (2 tablespoons) = 30 mL
4 fluid ounces (1/2 cup) = 125 mL
8 fluid ounces (1 cup) = 250 mL
12 fluid ounces (1 1/2 cups) = 375 mL
16 fluid ounces (2 cups) = 500 mL

## WEIGHTS (mass)

1/2 ounce = 15 g
1 ounce = 30 g
3 ounces = 90 g
4 ounces = 120 g
8 ounces = 225 g
10 ounces = 285 g
12 ounces = 360 g
16 ounces = 1 pound = 450 g

## DIMENSIONS

1/16 inch = 2 mm
1/8 inch = 3 mm
1/4 inch = 6 mm
1/2 inch = 1.5 cm
3/4 inch = 2 cm
1 inch = 2.5 cm

## OVEN TEMPERATURES

250°F = 120°C
275°F = 140°C
300°F = 150°C
325°F = 160°C
350°F = 180°C
375°F = 190°C
400°F = 200°C
425°F = 220°C
450°F = 230°C

## BAKING PAN SIZES

| Utensil | Size in Inches/Quarts | Metric Volume | Size in Centimeters |
|---|---|---|---|
| Baking or | 8×8×2 | 2 L | 20×20×5 |
| Cake Pan | 9×9×2 | 2.5 L | 23×23×5 |
| (square or | 12×8×2 | 3 L | 30×20×5 |
| rectangular) | 13×9×2 | 3.5 L | 33×23×5 |
| Loaf Pan | 8×4×3 | 1.5 L | 20×10×7 |
| | 9×5×3 | 2 L | 23×13×7 |
| Round Layer | 8×1½ | 1.2 L | 20×4 |
| Cake Pan | 9×1½ | 1.5 L | 23×4 |
| Pie Plate | 8×1¼ | 750 mL | 20×3 |
| | 9×1¼ | 1 L | 23×3 |
| Baking Dish | 1 quart | 1 L | — |
| or Casserole | 1½ quart | 1.5 L | — |
| | 2 quart | 2 L | — |